ISRAEL

Designed and Produced by
Ted Smart & David Gibbon

COLOUR LIBRARY BOOKS

Introduction

Israel is a unique combination of the very ancient and the ultra-modern, of idealism and pragmatism. The country and its people cannot properly be appreciated without some understanding of their history, however condensed.

Israel has been battled for, ruled by, a dozen diverse powers during the ages preceding the state's foundation: external influences have played a great role in moulding her character – an intense nationalism tempered by a cosmopolitan outlook.

The biblical story of the Land of Israel is familiar to millions of people: it is part of the monotheism shared by three great religions.

After the Return (538 BC) from Babylonian exile, the Jews experienced a resurgence of independence, interrupted by constant warfare. The Romans conquered the territory (63 BC) and, after the great revolt against them of AD 66-70, they destroyed the Second Temple in Jerusalem. Fresh exile was the fate of many Israelites.

Another insurrection (AD 132) resulted in further dispersions. Although there was always a Jewish presence, however small, in the Homeland – preserving the old religion and Rabbinical Law – the mainstream of Jewish life was for centuries outside the Holy Land.

By the early 19th century, the population of what is now Israel had fallen catastrophically. It required very great faith for a Jew – whether he was prospering in a tolerant state, suffering harsh repression under hostile government or surviving as an oppressed minority in his own God-given country – to believe that a mass Return to an independent homeland was more than a mystical dream, perhaps to be realised by remote generations yet scarcely conceivable in any foreseeable future.

Then came the humble beginnings of what, within under a century, was to develop into the State of Israel. In 1878, a small party of pioneers from Jerusalem founded a new type of Jewish community, a farm village (Petach Tikva). Jews commenced, against all odds, to come in small, but growing, numbers to the Promised Land. Their movement, watched with hope by thousands unable to attempt such a journey, was formalised by Theodor Herzl, an Austrian journalist. He transformed Zionism from an age-old yearning, a creed of expectation, into a forceful political aim. In August, 1887, the first Zionist Congress convened in Basle.

Zionism became an international force, its supporters and its enemies numbering both Jews and non-Jews. Fired by the Zionist ideal, often financed by Jews abroad, increasing numbers from countries where anti-Semitism was rife made hazardous journeys joyously to face the rigours of life in Palestine, which had become a decaying backwater of the doomed Ottoman empire. That corrupt entity was demolished after World War I, during which the British, who liberated Jerusalem, affirmed, by the polemical Balfour Declaration, sympathy for the establishment of a Jewish state. In 1922, the League of Nations granted Britain a mandate to rule Palestine. This resulted in the formation of an Arab Trans-Jordania, leaving only a quarter of Palestine as an embryonic Jewish National Home.

There was constant and often bloody friction between the protecting power, the Jews and the Arabs. After World War II came terrorism, counter-terror, massacre and reprisal. Jews continued to arrive in thousands, mainly illegally, to establish settlements and to defend them. Britain, discouraged by a man-in-the-middle role, in 1947 turned the turbulent region over to the United Nations. The UN re-partitioned the country, giving much

Outside the Knesset – the seat of the Israeli Parliament – stands Benno Elkan's Menorah left, *carved with scenes from Jewish history.*

Overleaf *stands the 'Jewel Box of Islam' – the Dome of the Rock – at the heart of Jerusalem's Old City.*

less to the Jews than they would have liked but establishing a formal Jewish state of sorts for the first time. Reluctantly, particularly on the issue of Jerusalem, the Jews accepted this arrangement. However, the Arabs scorned anything which admitted a separate Jewish presence and sporadic violence against Jewish communities erupted. In May, 1948, Britain thankfully evacuated her armed forces: Israel proclaimed herself a sovereign state. This led to full-scale war: six Arab armies invaded Israel with the intention of settling the issue finally.

The Arabs were quickly and very decisively beaten. An astonished and, for the most part, admiring world recognised the new State of Israel by admitting her to the United Nations in 1949. Theodor Herzl's vision was at last an actuality, and Jews flocked freely into Israel.

Israel has had to endure further battles to preserve her existence: those conflicts are part of the story of our times.

Land

Israel is at the crossroads of east and west, and, from north to south, between Asia and Africa. Jerusalem is 5,600 miles from New York; over 2,000 from London; 1,700 from Frankfurt; 8,750 from Sydney; 5,600 from Tokyo; 7,500 from Buenos Aires, and 1,600 from Moscow.

Though not as large as the U.S. state of Maine, Israel is extraordinarily diverse geographically and climatically. In the north are lush valleys, rivers and lakes and snow-capped mountains. To the south are deserts as arid as the Sahara. Yet revival of ancient irrigation systems, and installation of new ones, are revitalising neglected regions and again bringing an era of milk-and-honey to places that have for centuries been sandy wastelands. By ingenious use of water from the fertile north, the amount of cultivated land in the south has increased sixfold since 1948.

There is the amazing phenomenon of the Dead Sea, the lowest spot on earth, 1,296 feet below sea level. However, it is not entirely a dead sea: indeed there may be no fish, but it has marvellous curative powers, is a tourist resort of some consequence and maintains a rich, chemical industry.

The rainfall in Jerusalem averages 19 inches annually: it is slightly higher in Tel Aviv. At Eilat on the Red Sea a mere 1 inch falls. Respective temperatures are: Jerusalem – (August) C.19-28, F.64-82; (January) C.5-12, F.41-54. Tel Aviv –(August) C.22-30, F.72-86; (January) C.11-20, F.52-68. Eilat – (August) C.20-33, F.68-92; (January) C.11-23, F.52-73.

People

When the state of Israel was declared in 1948, the population was 800,000: it is now well over 3,600,000. (Figures exclude disputed areas.) This is certainly more than for the whole vaster region once known as Palestine at its most flourishing. It is estimated that following successive diasporas, the collapse of irrigation, and constant futile wars for domination of the region, by the mid-16th century the country could have supported no more than 200,000.

Today, 85% of Israeli citizens are Jews, 12% Moslems, just over 2% Christian and the remainder are Druze or belong to tiny ethnic or religious groups. Israeli Jews include anyone so designating themselves, whether native-born (Sabra) – over 50% of the total – or immigrants from abroad. Legally, the term Jew is without religious significance: it embraces members of Orthodox or heretic sects; the secular, agnostic or atheistic, alongside the pious. The term Israeli is nationalist, not racial. People of singularly diversified physical types, originating in many lands, are uniformly proud to be Jews and Israelis. Thus Israeli citizenship

enfolds the genius of people from an immense spectrum of humanity, and this accounts for Israel's abounding enterprise, stamina, intellectual energy and cultural diversity. Israel is, above all, a nation founded on adversity. The will of her people has been forged in misfortune, refined by tragedy, sharpened by an ideal, and enlivened by quest for survival. The long-sought national heritage has brought together a warrior people, yet devoted to peace and progress, who have earned their nationhood and cherish it with peculiar fierceness. Thus, just as Israel welcomes new citizens, she likes to play host to anyone who simply wants to come and see what she has done, to share her past and to enjoy her particular fascination. She invites with equal warmth the historian, the scholar, the holiday-maker and carefree tourist, and the businessman.

The principal minority, the Arabs (Moslems) have increased from 156,000, when the state was founded, to around 444,000. They hold all rights of full Israeli citizenship. Few pursue the archaic nomadic life of their forebears, preferring to take part in the benefits of the expanding economy, urban or rural. Any notion of a depressed Arab community is dispelled by two simple statistics: 75% of their households have refrigerators and 70% possess television sets.

Cities

Though for historical reasons the outside world tends to think of Israel as a pastoral country – citrus estates and olive groves, vineyards and sheep flocks – in fact 85% of all Israelis live in cities or towns. In addition there are many villages, some of considerable size, including kibbutzim and moshavim. No less than 500 villages and minor towns have been built since 1948 and most of these, founded by newly arrived citizens, are in the mountains or reclaimed deserts.

A very high proportion of Israelis inhabit the Mediterranean coastal belt. The greatest single concentration is in Tel Aviv and its suburbs – over 1 million. The capital, Jerusalem, has 366,000 inhabitants. On the coast, the second biggest city is Haifa in the north (227,000). The most southerly city is the vital port, and popular winter Red Sea resort, of Eilat (17,000). Major conurbations include Ashkelon (49,000) – southernmost of Mediterranean cities – and neighbouring Ashdod (55,000); Beersheba (99,000); Nazareth (57,000); Natanya (86,000), and Rishon Le Zion (73,000).

Moshavim

A moshav is a co-operative village of smallholders, combining collective farming with private enterprise. Though much less publicised than the famous kibbutzim, more people occupy moshavim (over 135,000) than are members of kibbutzim (103,000).

In 1948 there were only 58 moshavim and 149 kibbutzim, whereas the figures are now 377 and 300. There is not much in common between the two systems.

The moshav principle is popular and it plays an important part in the national economy. In a moshav, each family has its own house, farms its own land and manages its own funds. The moshav owns and maintains agricultural machinery, purchases materials to the best advantage of members and conducts the marketing of produce. A few moshavim engage in industry and in some instances combine with other villages to make a more efficient unit.

In 1953, David Ben-Gurion, one of the architects of modern Israel, made his modest home at Sde Boker Kibbutz and it is here, overlooking the Negev Desert left that he lies buried, together with his wife Paula.

In Jerusalem's Old City stand the assortment of buildings overleaf that, together, make up the Church of the Holy Sepulchre.

The rise of the moshavim owes much to the character of a large section of post-war immigrants, many of whom detested the socialism of the kibbutzim, wanting more freedom and the chance to see the results of their individual efforts. At first the government tried to integrate members of new moshavim from various countries, but it was found that immigrants much preferred to work alongside people who shared their language and background, so that scheme was abandoned and folk of similar cultures were put together, leaving it to second generation moshavim members to merge with those of different communities.

So successful have moshavim been that Israeli experts have been invited to set up similar organisations in developing countries.

Kibbutzim

The kibbutz is probably the one feature of Israel familiar to foreigners who know nothing else about the country. For some time this institution has engaged the interest of the outside world. The kibbutz was crucial in the early stages of Israel's formation.

Though kibbutzim vary greatly in age, size, prosperity, activity and location, the basic principle is always the same. They are an expression of voluntary, practical socialism – communism if you like – not practised anywhere else on a similar scale. Members of a kibbutz receive no money, in effect possess nothing of their own. All services, from food to clothing, are communal; everything is provided by the kibbutz according to need and the facilities of the commune. Children are in communal care. All work, on farm, in workshop, kitchens or laundry, is shared and no hired help is used – which has sometimes created problems. Profits are ploughed back into further development. Members of kibbutzim, heirs to the eight persons who started the first one in 1909, want to live this way – for part of their lives in any event. No one coerces them.

All members of a kibbutz meet weekly to discuss community affairs, to consider admissions, and to elect, as occasion arises, such officers as secretary, treasurer and works manager, who serve for two years. Elected committees oversee every aspect of kibbutz life from sport to education.

At first, kibbutzim were wholly agricultural but nowadays most manufacture a wide range of articles. Life is still tough in some, even dangerous, yet despite their anti-capitalist philosophy and hostility to personal gain, kibbutzim are by no means necessarily the spartan places of legend. Provided they are communal, it does not offend members of successful kibbutzim to enjoy modern amenities, even luxuries, gained by their own hard work for the common good.

Kibbutzniks, past and present, have provided a disproportionate number of officers for the defence forces: in the Six Day War, one in four casualties was a kibbutznik. Though only about 3% of the population, members of kibbutzim wield considerable political muscle as supporters of various left-wing parties. By their nature, modern kibbutzniks tend not to be particularly religious. However, eleven kibbutzim adhere to an extreme Orthodox Jewish group and are affiliated to the strict National Religious Party.

From overseas, young single people, or married couples without children, between the ages 18-32, can visit kibbutzim for a variety of serious work/study schemes.

Industry

Israel is effectively self-supporting in food and is a major exporter of agricultural produce, notably citrus fruit and out-of-season vegetables, all of the highest quality, to Europe in particular. Heavy industry includes steel, miscellaneous machinery, aircraft, ships, electronic and science-related products, synthetic textiles, diamond finishing and mineral processing. Amongst leading consumer products are processed foods, fashion wear, leather

goods, furniture, electrical apparatus, jewellery, religious objects and books. Tourism is an important industry.

Defence

Israel's defence forces (IDF) are rightly held in high esteem. Their core is a small body of professionals, mostly officers with specialised knowledge. There is universal conscription at the age of 18: 36 months for men and 24 for women. Deferments can be obtained for students and exemptions may be granted on health grounds, or for reasons of conscience: there are very seldom applications in the latter category. Thus an extremely efficient, and dedicated, corps of reservists has been built up. IDF reservists usually do a month's training a year. Men remain on the reserve, health permitting, until 55 and women until 34, but married women are rarely recalled to service. National service in the IDF has had the beneficial side-effect of integrating people of widely differing origins into a cohesive Israeli society.

Food

Many non-Jews relish kosher food, whilst numerous Jews do not strictly abide by the laws concerning its preparation and serving. In Israel there is no legislation concerning kosher food: it is left entirely to the individual to be as lax or orthodox as is liked. Most hotels are kosher, but plenty of restaurants are not.

Apart from certain prohibitions, there is nothing the gastronome need fear in using kosher establishments. Jewish cooking has long been famed for its tastiness – and quantity.

The rules concerning kosher food are of clear biblical origin and their purpose was originally to maintain health through commonsense rules in a hostile climate. Ritual has complicated the matter. As to meat, the animal must not have cloven hooves. Thus beef is permissible, but not pork. Fish must have both scales and fins: that rules out eel or shellfish. A meal which includes meat must not also have a butter or milk content; so a kosher dinner of steak cannot be followed by coffee with cream. This stems from a traditional interpretation of biblical canons. Kosher kitchens should have a set of utensils, crockery and cutlery for meat meals, and a separate one for dairy products. To satisfy modern taste without offending kosher rules, in Israel an excellent "ice cream" has been evolved from egg whites, which may be taken after meat.

Animals must be killed by a humane ritual slaughter which obviously originated to ensure that nothing but fresh meat was eaten. The carcase has to be examined to see that the beast was healthy.

The non-Jewish visitor to Israel will be put to no inconvenience. Jews can be assured of whatever degree of observance of kosher rules they desire.

Other cuisines abound – Levantine, Arabic, French, Russian, German – or international menus, including American "fast foods".

Wine

Not only does wine play an important ritual role in orthodox Jewish life, but Israelis like wine. They produce a lot of it. Israel inherited a long, if disturbed, history of wine-making. Her land is part of former kingdoms rich in vineyards four thousand years ago or more. The region probably saw man's first use of the fermented juice of the grape. A prolonged period of Moslem domination considerably, but not entirely, eradicated Palestinian vineyards: the Ottomans were fairly tolerant about the making of

The miracle at Cana, where Jesus is said to have turned the water into wine, is simplistically treated in the Franciscan church left at Kfar Kana.

Beyond the towers and monuments overleaf in the Kidron Valley rises the Mount of Olives.

wine by their subject races and were rarely fanatical in the prohibition of alcohol.

Israel's wine industry started a century ago when immigrant Jews took advantage of Rothschild generosity to plant vines on some of the meagre acres allotted them for agriculture. A small production had commenced when the phylloxera plague that had ravaged European vines arrived in the Middle East on its worldwide tour of destruction. Again, in 1882, Rothschild philanthropy came to the rescue, re-stocking the fields with phylloxera-resistant American roots that had saved other winelands. By 1909, the wine industry was sufficiently prosperous for Baron Edmond de Rothschild to hand over to the growers the wineries he had established at Rishon-Le Zion (Tel Aviv region) and Zichron-Ya'acov (south of Haifa). A co-operative was formed which, under state control, now produces 75% of all Israeli wines and is virtually the sole exporter.

Wine has been sent to Britain since the turn of the century, but today three-quarters of Israel's wine exports go to the United States (about 15% of the production). In Israel you will find not just the sweet white wines particularly associated with the country but those of all types, and of good quality, including excellent sparkling varieties, also local liqueurs of which one (Sabra) has become extremely popular in West Germany.

Wine is made under Rabbinical supervision. Some Christian pastors indeed insist that their sacramental wine comes from the Holy Land.

VISITOR'S ISRAEL
Jerusalem (Yerushalayim)

The focal point of Israel is Jerusalem. It is much more than the capital. It is not just set in the heart of the country: it is the country's heart. And, as well as that, its importance in Christianity is vital; for many Moslems it is their third holiest city.

To Jews no place is more sacred than Jerusalem's Western Wall, colloquially the Wailing Wall. The Romans obliterated the great Temple which King Herod had enlarged and redecorated (19 BC), but they left one cyclopean wall of the Temple compound. During later centuries, Jews were only allowed into Jerusalem once a year to lament the destruction of the Temple by praying at the Western Wall, which became a symbol of Jews' hopes. Not until 1967 were their prayers fully answered, with unrestricted access to the Wall.

The original Jerusalem, city of David, who made it his capital after capturing it in 1004 BC, was south of the present city. Archaeologists think they may have uncovered the tunnel through which King David made his way into the city. He is remembered in many ways; his musical attainments, well documented in the Bible, are commemorated in the International Harp Contest, a feature of modern Jerusalem's active, cultural life.

A short selection of principal points of interest in Israel, divided into three regions, indicates how wide are the country's attractions.

Northern Region

Haifa – Third largest city. Main port and industrial centre. Summer resort on Mount Carmel. Good base for Galilee tours.
Acre (Akko) – Important city since Phoenician era; full of historic relics.
Deganya – First ever kibbutz (1909), near Sea of Galilee and River Jordan.
En Hod – Colourful artists' village near Haifa.
Golan Heights – Druze villages, and interesting settlements maintained by energetic young Israelis.
Hammath Gader – Ancient spa with hot springs and Roman antiquities.
Mount (Har) Hermon – Towering over Golan Heights plateau.

Ski resort, with accommodation in moshav.

Mount Tabor – Site of Christ's Transfiguration.

Mount Carmel (Har Karmel) – Carmelite monastery. Country's largest National Park.

Hazor – Very important archaeological sites.

Cana – Traditional site of Christ's first miracle, the changing of water into wine at the wedding feast.

Capernaum – On the shore of Sea of Galilee; strong Christian associations.

Belvoir–12th-century Crusaders' castle perched above Jordan.

Meggido – Major archaeological site in Jezreel Valley, said to be site of King Solomon's stables. Christian mythology maintains this will be where Armageddon takes place.

Mount of Beatitudes – Overlooking Sea of Galilee, where Sermon on the Mount is said to have been preached.

Nazareth – Childhood home of Christ, replete with Christian shrines.

Tabgha – Sea of Galilee; traditional placing of miracle of the Loaves and Fishes. Fine Byzantine church.

Tiberias – On shores of Sea of Galilee; founded 2,000 years ago to honour Caesar Tiberius. One of four Holy Cities of Israel; pilgrimage centre. Winter resort noted for hot springs.

Zichron-Ya'acov – Grape-growing area near Haifa; wine-making. Visits to cellars. Rothschild mausoleum.

Central Region

Jerusalem

Tel Aviv – Financial, cultural and modern social centre. Museums and art galleries. Large hotel area on sea frontage. Open-air cafés and restaurants. Bustling metropolis with fine beaches close at hand.

Jaffa (Yafo) – Ancient port, incorporated into Tel Aviv. Fine reconstructions in old city.

Ashkelon – One of ancient Philistine city states; associated with Samson. Roman and, for a time, Crusader town. Resort, with National Park containing many antiquities; camping grounds.

Bethlehem – Birthplace of Christ and of King David. Christian shrines, also Arab market-place.

Hebron – Holy City; Tombs of the Patriarchs.

Natanya – Important Mediterranean resort town. Centre of diamond-cutting industry.

Caesarea – Extensive Roman ruins and finely rebuilt theatre. Crusader relics. Resort town, with golf course.

Qumran – Archaeological centre on Dead Sea; Scrolls were found nearby.

Rehovot – South of Tel Aviv. Centre of citrus fruit belt. Burial-place of Chaim Weizman, Israel's first president, and site of Institute of Sciences named after him. Hebrew University's Faculty of Agriculture.

Rishon-Le Zion – First settlement by pioneers of 1882 (the Bilu movement). Splendid wineries.

Nablus – Biblical city north of Jerusalem. Samaritan religious centre. Jacob's Tomb and Well.

Jericho – Oasis in Jordan Valley and northern end of Dead Sea. Ruins of what is claimed as one of the world's oldest cities.

Southern Region

Beersheba – Modern city on spot where Abraham pitched his tent. Ben Gurion University.

Hai Bar – Biblical Wildlife Reserve north of Eilat.

Masada – Massive hill fortress where last Jewish survivors of revolt against Romans all died in AD 74 rather than surrender into

Spectacular arches in the Negev Desert left, hewn from the solid rock by the forces of nature over aeons of time.

Crowds start to gather overleaf in the late afternoon sun at the Western, or 'Wailing' Wall of the Temple.

slavery. Well restored; served by cable-car.

Sodom – Biblical twin town to Gomorrah, destroyed for their wickedness by Jehovah. Dead Sea potash processing.

Eilat – Popular winter seaside resorts. Remarkable facilities for aquatic observation and sports.

Kibbutz Inns

The chain of Kibbutz Inns, unique to Israel, offers an unusual and most agreeable way of visiting various parts of the country. It allows the traveller to witness aspects of kibbutz life without involvement in the kibbutzniks' work-ethic. Alternatively, Kibbutz Inns can just be used as hotels. (The term, for tourist purposes, covers a few establishments that are not strictly inns.) Primarily, Kibbutz Inns are run as commercial adjuncts to kibbutzim's communal commerce. They are sometimes referred to as guest houses, implying a simple attachment to a kibbutz farm, but so far as overseas visitors are concerned, most Kibbutz Inns are fine modern establishments. Out of 23 listed in the special GTO guidebook, 2 have official four-star rating and fifteen are three-star; 16 are fully kosher. Nearly all are air-conditioned, have big swimming-pools, and private bathrooms/showers are the rule rather than the exception. Numbers of rooms in the Inns ranges from 140 to around 55, so there is an intimacy not to be found in large, impersonal tourist hotels. Kibbutz Inns, all else apart, are frequently the best places in which to stay when visiting historic sites in the thirty or so National Parks of Israel; some are tourist resorts in their own right.

MISCELLANEOUS INFORMATION

Tourists must have PASSPORTS valid for Israel, and should check whether they need visas; also if vaccinations are required. Special visas needed for anyone seeking to work, study or settle in Israel.

There are no restrictions on the amount of CURRENCY that may be brought into the country. The currencies of a number of foreign countries may be used for purchases, though shops and services are not legally bound to accept them and may not exchange them for Israeli money.

The general rest day is Saturday, the Jewish SABBATH. Moslem shops and services close on Fridays and Christian establishments on Sunday.

The principal form of urban and inter-city public TRANSPORT is by bus. Public Transport does not run from sundown on Friday until Saturday nightfall. A taxi service (Sherut) takes passengers along fixed urban routes and also operates between many towns: for long distances seats may be reserved in advance. In cities there are conventional taxis with official tariffs. Some Sherut cars operate on the Sabbath. The internal airline, Arkia, flies on schedule between Jerusalem, Tel Aviv, Rosh Pina, Masada, Eilat and Sharm-el-Sheikh.

There are RAILWAYS from Nahariya in the north to Dimona in the south, and from Tel Aviv to Jerusalem: the latter is a scenic route. Fares are lower than for buses; refreshments are available on most trains.

SELF-DRIVE cars can be reserved through several inter-national companies, and arrangements made for them to be collected on arrival. Licences should be checked for validity in Israel.

TOURS are organised by several licensed operators. These are mainly by coach, but some are by limousine. Vehicles are usually air-conditioned. Tours range from half-day to three days and go regularly from Jerusalem, Tel Aviv and Haifa, and in high season from other cities. All tours are accompanied by official multi-lingual guides. There is a de-luxe service of 7-seater cars with driver-guides. Similar arrangements can be made for desert tours. Arkia has tours to Sinai and Eilat as well as package holidays. Walking tours are arranged by the Society for Protection of Nature. There are special interest tours for professional men, scientists, archaeologists and students.

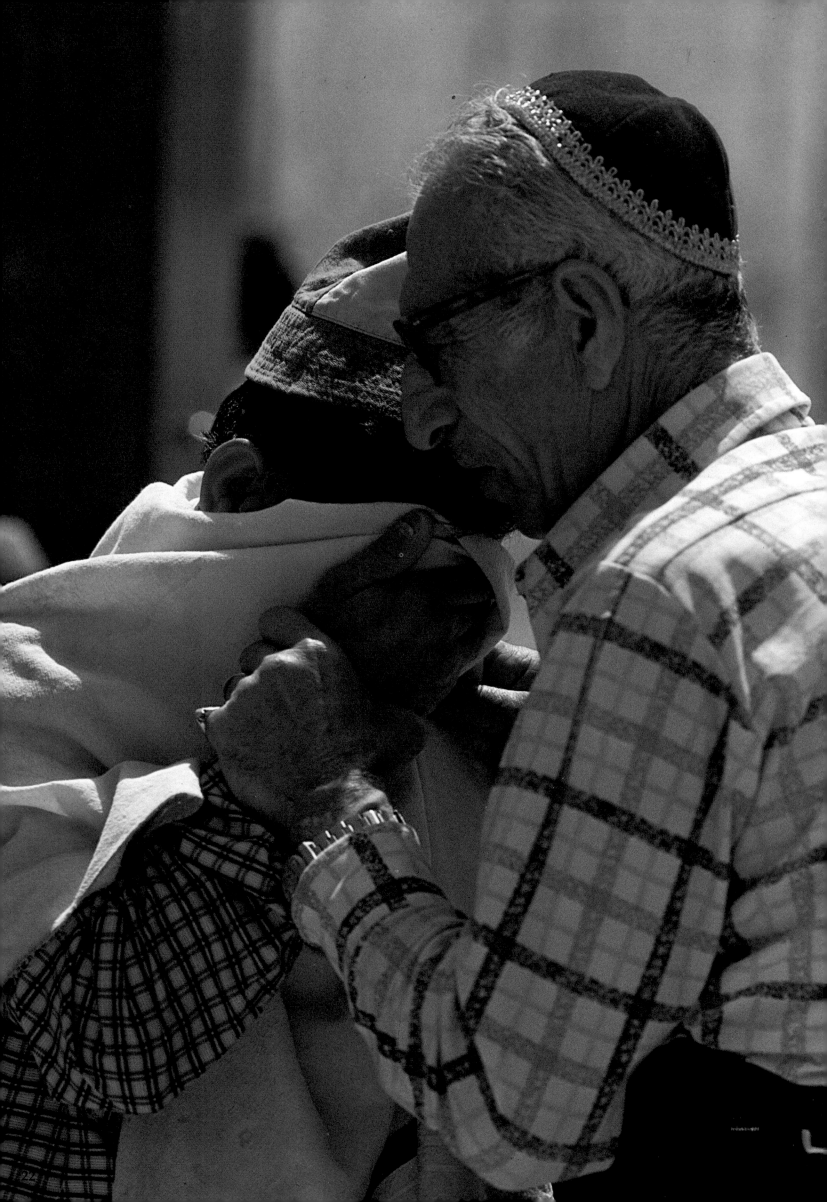

YOUTH HOSTELS exist throughout the country in association with the International Youth Hostels Association. A leaflet is obtainable from Israel GTOs or direct from IYHA, 3 Rehov Dorot Rishonim, Jerusalem. With particular appeal to the young are Holiday Villages.

Visitors who would like to stay in PRIVATE HOMES, if they have not made prior arrangements, may do so through information offices at Ben-Gurion Airport or in Jerusalem.

Christians on PILGRIMAGE can obtain accommodation at reasonable cost in the hospices of various denominations. Particulars from GTOs or from the Pilgrimage Committee, PO Box 1018, Jerusalem.

HOTELS are to international standards; they are available to suit every purse and preference. Prospective visitors are advised to obtain the latest booklet of the Israel Hotel Association. This is a useful reference for people travelling around the country. (See also Kibbutz Inns.)

The principal point of entry is Ben-Gurion International AIRPORT, Tel Aviv. Some shipping lines have passenger services from Europe to Haifa. The only feasible entry by land is from Jordan via the Allenby Bridge near Jericho.

Hebrew is the LANGUAGE of Israel, with Arabic used by 15% of the population. English is widely understood. The polyglot social mix is illustrated by the availability of 13 daily newspapers in 11 languages.

VALUE ADDED TAX is charged on all goods and services.

Apart from the most important, the Israel Museum in Jerusalem, leading MUSEUMS and ART GALLERIES are the Tel Aviv Museum, notable for its art exhibits, the Ha'Aretz Museum complex on the city's outskirts, and the Maritime Museum and the Museum Centre (old and modern art) at Haifa.

MUSIC plays a major role in cultural life. The most celebrated of several orchestras is the Israel Philharmonic which attracts leading conductors.

Israelis are amongst the world's keenest audiences for the THEATRE. Visitors with a knowledge of Hebrew should visit the Habimah and Cameri theatres in Tel Aviv or the Haifa municipal theatre. These companies also tour the country. Smaller companies perform in English and other languages.

Three principal BALLET companies tour the country – Israel Classical Ballet, and two modern dance ensembles, the Bat-Sheva and the Bat-Dor.

Various FESTIVALS are held regularly, and visitors with special interests may care to time their visits to coincide with them. The Israel Festival of Music and Drama (July and August) is centred on Jerusalem, with associated performances in Tel Aviv, the Roman auditorium at Caesarea and in some towns and large kibbutzim. The annual Ein Gev Music Festival takes place during Passover at the kibbutz of that name on the Sea of Galilee. Eilat has an exciting water sports festival. The International Harp Festival is a triennial event, as is the Zimirya International Choir Festival. 'Spring in Jerusalem,' including drama, music and dance, is held annually. The Rubinstein Piano Competition brings young talent from all over the world.

The CINEMA is popular in Israel: performances, usually three a day, start at about 4pm. RADIO programmes are broadcast daily in English, French, Yiddish and other languages. News is broadcast in English and French three times a day. TELEVISION is mainly conducted in Hebrew and Arabic, plus imported programmes. NIGHTCLUBS exist in cities and resort towns, a number featuring folk music, and informal cabarets, as well as the usual pop music. FOLKLORE evenings encapsulate the essence of Israel and help visitors understand the country in a special way: they are held regularly in Jerusalem, Tel Aviv, Haifa and Tiberias, and quite often in Ashkelon, Natanya and Eilat.

The Jerusalem Biblical ZOO is unusual in specialising in the many animals referred to in the Bible and there is a biblical wildlife reserve near Eilat, as well as a more conventional zoo. Tel Aviv has its own zoo. There is a Safari Park at Ramat Gan.

Arrangements can be made locally through any GTO for visitors to have social meetings with Israelis in their homes, to exchange news and views, and for professional people to be put in touch with Israelis with similar interests. Overseas members of international organisations such as Freemasons, B'Nai Brith, Rotary, Lions, Soroptimists, etc will find Israeli branches that are happy to welcome them.

Football and basketball are the premier Israeli sports. The Mediterranean and Sea of Galilee provide splendid water sports facilities. It is in the Eilat vicinity that aqualung diving is particularly good: equipment can be rented. Fishing equipment may be hired on the Mediterranean and at Eilat, though at the latter fishing is restricted. Many large hotels have tennis courts. Bicycles can be hired in many resorts and cycling tours are organised, a fine way to see the country. In winter there is skiing on Mount Hermon. There is an excellent 18-hole golf course at Caesarea. There are numerous camping sites.

Electricity supplies in Israel are on 220 volts AC, and some visitors' equipment, such as shavers, may need adapters, and also adapter-plugs to fit the three-prong sockets customarily in use.

Medical services are of a high order and most doctors speak English or other foreign languages. Free emergency dental treatment is available to visitors.

A symbol very widely seen is that of the Menorah emblem of the State. This seven-branched candelabrum goes back to the earliest days of Jewish history when it formed part of the furniture of the Tabernacle, built by the Children of Israel as they wandered in the wilderness after escaping from Egypt. Depictions of the emblem will be found everywhere – scratched in primitive style on clay tablets or in grandiose sculptural shape outside the Knesset.

An emotional scene left at the Wailing Wall.

Jerusalem – the 'City of Earth and Heaven' – overleaf seems just that as it lies, at night, shimmeringly bathed in soft, golden light.

The Dead Sea Scrolls, *discovered in a cave at Qumran* below, *are now housed in the magnificent Shrine of the Book* left *and* bottom.

Relatives and friends gather overleaf *for a Bar Mitzvah ceremony at the Western Wall.*

27

On the lower slopes of the Mount of Olives stands the impressively beautiful Gethsemane Church of All Nations *above and overleaf,* built on the site of two earlier churches and so-named because its building was sponsored by many different countries.

The Star of David *right* has been for countless years the symbol of Judaism.

In the Kidron Valley, which runs between Mount Ophel and the Mount of Olives, are several Second Temple Monuments, one of which, the so-called Absalom's Pillar, is shown *below.*

A timeless and strangely moving scene in the Old City *left.*

The immensity of the stone blocks that make up the Western Wall of the Temple, Judaism's holiest shrine, where Jews from all over the world gather to pray, may be judged from the pictures left, top, above and above right.

Written pleas and prayers are still pushed into the spaces between the great, ancient stones overleaf.

A Palm Sunday procession makes its way through the streets of the Old City right.

Floodlighting bathes the old stones of Jerusalem's Monastery of the Cross above.

Three of the holiest shrines of three great religions: the Western Wall of the Temple left and below, the main entrance to the Church of the Holy Sepulchre right, and the bare rock overlea that lies at the heart of the Dome of the Rock on the Temple Mount.

Contrasts in architectural styles: a soft glow fills the beautiful Church of All Nations right at Gethsemane, while further up the slope of the Mount of Olives rise the characteristically Russian, onion-shaped domes above of the Eastern Orthodox Church of Mary Magdalene.

The bells of the Tomb of the Virgin are shown below, and left is the view over Jerusalem from inside the lovely church called Dominus Flevit – the Lord Wept – about halfway up the Mount of Olives.

West of the Old City overleaf stands the impressive John F. Kennedy Memorial above left.

The old and the new in Jerusalem. Outside the wall that flanks the blocked-up Golden Gate – Gate of Mercy – are the tombs of the Moslem cemetery above.

Adjoining the city's Jaffa Gate is the Citadel below and right, also known as David's Tower which was once the fortress guarding the palace Herod the Great.

In contrast is the eloquent Hall of Remembra left, a memorial commemorating the millions o Jews who perished in the European Holocaust.

A tributary of the Jordan River in the Golan Heights overleaf.

46

At the Wailing Wall the sexes are strictly segregated by dividing panels above.

The incredibly beautiful interior left and equally marvellously decorated exterior right of the Dome of the Rock.

In a restful setting outside the city's Damascus Gate is the Garden Tomb below, while overleaf is shown the barren wilderness of the Negev Desert.

Girls recruited into the Israeli Armed Forces the pages undergo very similar training to the men and receive instruction in all manner of modern weaponry including tanks.

With equal amounts of imagination, hard work and irrigation, crops as well as various species of desert cactus overleaf are able to thrive in the seemingly inhospitable Negev Desert.

Agriculture plays an extremely important part in the economy of Israel and, thanks to massive irrigation projects, the barren desert has been made to bloom again and to bear an abundance of crops these pages, particularly in the many kibbutz and in the area of the Galilee.

A sea of barley overleaf ready for harvesting, near Afula.

Recently excavated, the ruins of the hill-top fortress of Masada right are strongly evocative of the last, desperate stand made by the Jews against the forces of Rome in this mountain stronghold in AD 73.

The magnificent view from the top of Mount Tabor, near Nazareth, is shown overleaf, and left the view from Ben Gurion's tomb in the Negev Desert.

South of Beersheba stands the monument below to the Six Day War.

To float above on, rather than in, the waters of the Dead Sea is a quite unique experience.

*The remarkable fortress at Masada is featured left
and top; above right the Negev Brigade
Memorial; below is Avdat, the first of the
Nabatean towns to be restored. Caesarea right
and above has provided archaeologists with
endless opportunities to delve into the area's past.
Stalactites and stalagmites overleaf in Sorek
Cave, Absalom's Reserve.*

Street markets throughout the Middle East have an obvious similarity as these pictures taken in Acre *right*, Beersheba *below* and *overleaf left*, and Jerusalem *overleaf right*, *show*.

Two Arab women pass the time of day *left* in Awarta, on the West Bank, and *above* is a Bedouin family with all its animals and belongings near the shores of the Red Sea.

*the previous page is a view across Nazareth,
he Galilee, where Jesus spent much of his
dhood.
he subject of veneration by countless Christian
rims throughout the ages is the Silver Star left,
he grotto of the Church of the Nativity in
hlehem this page and overleaf, while dawn
gs its soft, pink glow to the landscape below
ht.*

Ruins at Armageddon above and right – the 'Hills of Megiddo'– where, according to the Bible the last battle of the world will be fought.

Left is shown the remains of Castle Nimrod, Crusader Castle in the Golan Heights, and below is a palm tree carving that forms part of t remains of the synagogue at Capernaum.

Overleaf may be seen the sweeping view over the rooftops of Nazareth.

Above left: *boats at their moorings in the harbour of the popular holiday resort of Eilat.*
    The Cave of the Seventy Elders is shown bottom, *and its interior* below.
    In Tiberias stands the tomb of Rabbi Meir B Haness above, *and the old city wall at the water edge* below left.
    Basking in the clear, Mediterranean sunlight lies Acre's Fisherman's Harbour right *and* overleaf.

el Aviv left, top right, overleaf and following
ages *is the largest city in Israel. It is a fast-*
rowing and modern city that now includes in its
oundaries the ancient port of Jaffa.

For 600 years Caesarea centre right *was the*
apital of the Roman province of Judea, and much
it has now been excavated and restored.

Inland from the Sea of Galilee stands the lovely
Church of the Beatitudes below.

Bottom right are shown the old, sea-pounded
rtifications at Acre, and above *on the coast*
uth of Acre, at Rosh Ha 'Nikra – the Ladder of
yre – the waves sometimes rush and roar through
e many rock caverns and passages.

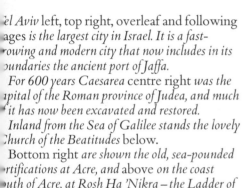

89